THE NAUTICAL STYLE

Frontispiece: Whitehaven, Cumberland, one of William Daniell's fine aquatints from Voyage Round Great Britain *(1814–25). A number of elements of the Nautical Style is here in its firm and functional geometry: the sea-wall, the quay, the lighthouse, the bollard.*

To six Eye-Openers, with respect:

John Piper

Sir James Richards

Hubert de Cronin Hastings

Gordon Cullen

Sir John Betjeman

Sir Nikolaus Pevsner

THE NAUTICAL STYLE

AN ASPECT OF THE FUNCTIONAL TRADITION

BY ERIC DE MARÉ

ARCHITECTURAL PRESS

ISBN 0 85139 447 7

First published 1973 by Architectural Press Ltd,

© Eric de Maré 1973

Photoset by Filmtype Services Limited, Scarborough,
and printed in England by Whitstable Litho, Whitstable, Kent.

CONTENTS

1. Definition   7

2. Sea-walls, Piers and Harbours   21

3. Warehouses, Docks and Special Structures   32

4. Lighthouses   45

5. On Inland Waters   61

6. Sculpture by Accident   71

7. Where Boats and Buildings Meet   81

Mid-eighteenth century compass card.

ACKNOWLEDGEMENTS

Excepting those listed below, all photographs are by the author, and all engravings come from the Maré Collection:

End papers, Peter Cornelius. Compass card, p. 5, Science Museum. Old ship, p.8, Science Museum. Stern of ship, p.10, National Maritime Museum. Blackpool pier, p.24, N Groves-Raines. Sea-wall, p.27, Roger Mayne. Sandgate sea-wall, p.27, I de Wolfe. The Cobb, Lyme Regis, p.28, top left, H de Burgh Galwey; bottom left, Ian McCallum; bottom right, H de Burgh Galwey; p.29 Gordon Cullen. Coastguard tower, p.42, C K Bowers & Sons. Sailing club, p.43, Keith Gibson. Harwich lighthouse, p.46, National Monuments Record. St Agnes lighthouse, p.46, Douglas B Hague. Mediaeval lighthouse, IOW, p.47, Roger Clark. Flamborough lighthouse, p.54, E R Yorks for NMR. St Anne's lighthouse, p.55, Douglas B Hague. Needles lighthouse, p.56, Roger Clark. Burnham lighthouse, p.57, Douglas B Hague. St Catherine's lighthouse, IOW, p.58, Roger Clark. Dungeness lighthouse, p.59, H de Burgh Galwey. Townscape drawings, p.68–9, Gordon Cullen. Husks, Holy Island, p.82, Edwin Johnston. Launching cradle, p.83, Stewart Bale. Bessemer saloon, p.84, Radio Times Hulton Picture Library. Luxury suite, QE2, p.87, Henk Snoek.

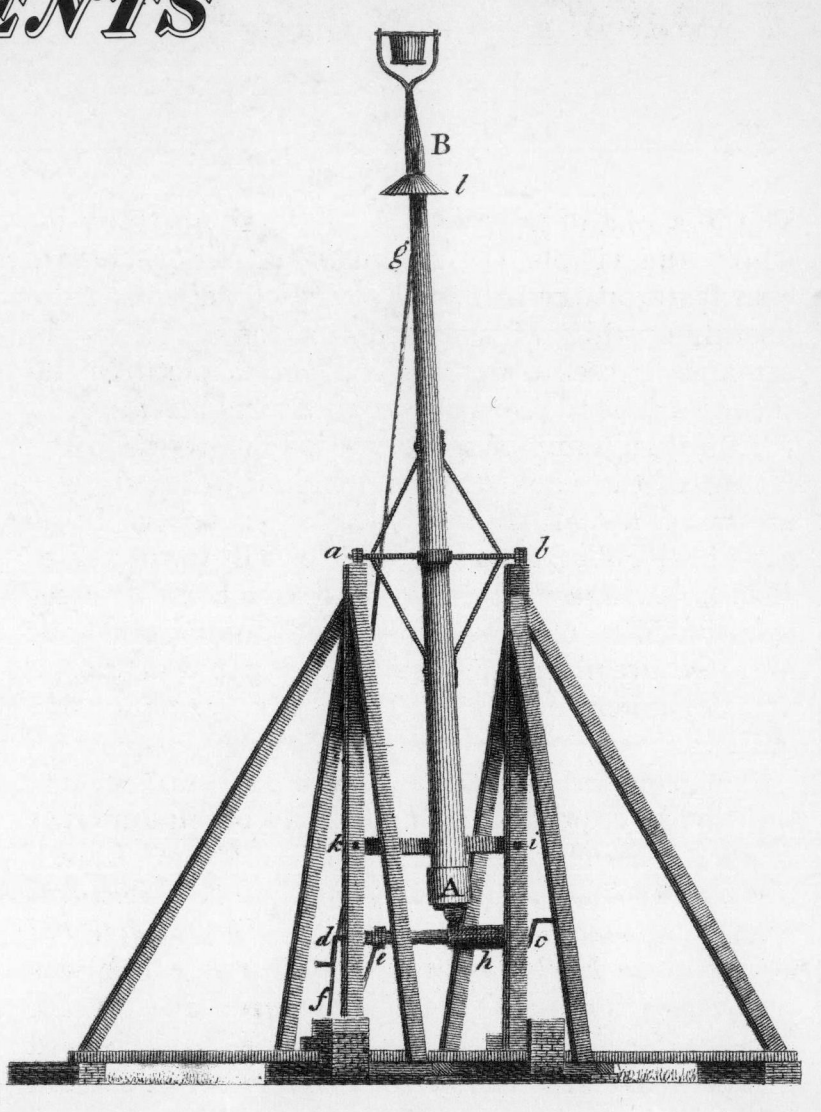

The Swape, or low light machine, on Spurn Point at the mouth of the Humber, an engraving from Smeaton's Narrative of the Building of the Edystone Lighthouse *(1813). The light came from a basket of coal raised and lowered by rope.*

1 DEFINITION

The first aim of this book is to please all those for whom the visible world exists and whose hearts beat faster at the primeval sound of waves and the nostalgic whiff of seaweed and ozone. It is an attempt to create a sort of poem in pictures. Its second aim is to point an architectural moral.

Although many of the photographs here and the layout of the book and its compilation in stanzas are mine, not all the ideas expressed are so. Some have been culled from the pages of the *Architectural Review,* a magazine which has through the decades formulated a number of stimulating ideas about architecture in the broadest meaning of that abused and misunderstood word. This work enshrines one of them.

That unadorned functionalism was not merely the rebellious product of the 'thirties but has ancient roots is one of the notions born at Queen Anne's Gate. In 1957 a special number of the *Architectural Review* appeared under the title *The Functional Tradition in Early Industrial Buildings* which was the joint effort of Sir James Richards and myself. A year later it was published as a book that achieved a certain *succès d'estime* at a time when a sudden new interest was developing in industrial archaeology. Here is an addendum that covers a particularly attractive category of the tradition.

Sir James wrote in the former volume: "Because of all the misunderstandings that have grown up round the term 'functionalism', in the heat of the struggle to establish its supremacy over the philosophy that survived from the nineteenth century, when pictorial and antiquarian values predominated, functionalism has acquired the reputation of being a revolutionary creed peculiar to our day . . . It is nothing of the sort."

Through architectural history there is a continuous thread running with the historical styles but owing nothing to them – as, for example, in the military works of the Middle Ages that possess the bold simplicity engendered by overriding functional considerations. Its elements are geometry unadorned, and it owes its effects to the forthright, spare and logical use of materials. It emerges strongly in the buildings of the Industrial Revolution, not least in the splendid engineering structures that gave the Revolution its impetus before engineering and architecture so foolishly decided on divorce.

7

From such buildings we, who also live in an age when functional qualities are highly valued, can learn a lot.

The examples in this book of maritime structures

The term Nautical Style as here defined does not include ship design, old or new, such as the late sixteenth century example under construction above (from the Pepysian Library), or the modern Clydeside example on the facing page.

and artifacts with their uncompromising purposes support the argument. For centuries in the countryside a rural tradition of functionalism has existed that has answered practical needs (not least in wind and water mills) with rightness and economy. Its progeny were not intended to form picturesque and endearing objects in the landscape by those who designed and built them; they had important jobs to do. Like this rural tradition is the nautical tradition of the coasts and waterways. Its products are often bold, sometimes graceful, sometimes grand in scale, and always as efficient, economical, honest and comely in construction and appropriate use of materials as the dancing creations of the age-old craft of the shipwright they exist to serve.

The beauty achieved has never been the deliberate aim of the designers, most of whom have remained unknown and unsung, for an enviable unselfconsciousness marks the entire Functional Tradition. That is a virtue we have lost. As an old cartwright, last of his breed, replied with a scratch of his head when an urban designer asked him how he achieved such formal perfection in his hay wains: "I dunno; I just makes 'em right." Pure Zen. We cannot recapture such innocence and perhaps therein lies the modern tragedy; we know too much and can do too much. And we lack the disciplines that produce the aesthetic of an established vernacular; we lack in particular the rooted discipline developed by centuries of slow, meticulous growth.

The special need of architecture now is the initiation of a fresh vernacular grammar, appropriate to our times, in which the best ideas of all the innovators are incorporated and merged. That is not easy to accomplish in this corrupt, unstable and self-conscious age, an age that has become utterly enslaved by the absurd and abused abstractions of money. The first step towards such a grammar must be a striving to maintain the true functional tradition and to revolt now with help of plain words against asinine, and sycophantic pretensions and mystiques.

The Nautical Style persists, as a number of modern structures reveal (a few of them shown here). For you cannot fool the elements; you cannot play games with the sea – nor, indeed, with the ferocious force of water trying to find the tranquility of its own level in any place. When dealing with realities that can kill you have to build 'em right.* From such

---

*I cannot resist quoting an extract here from Conrad's *An Outcast of the Islands:* "The sea, perhaps because of its saltness, roughens the outside but keeps sweet the kernel of its servant's soul. The old sea; the sea of many years ago, whose servants were devoted slaves and went from youth to age or to a sudden grave without needing to open the book of life, because they could look at eternity reflected in the element that gave the life and dealt the death. Like a beautiful and unscrupulous woman, the sea of the past was glorious in its smiles, irresistible in its anger, capricious, illogical, irresponsible: a thing to love, a thing to fear. It cast a spell, it gave joy, it lulled gently into boundless faith; then with quick and causeless anger it killed. But its cruelty was redeemed by the charm of its inscrutable mystery, by the immensity of its promise, by the supreme witchery of its possible favour. Strong men with childlike hearts were faithful to it, were content to live by its grace – to die by its will."

integrity arise forms that always display a robust, sculptural vigour. Jolly decoration for its own playful sake is eschewed; yet decorative effects are often achieved incidentally in such a vernacular – in the rhythmical repetition of elements, for example, or in the rich textures of natural materials, or in contrasts of bright colours and of tones (not least of black and white). That true functionalism produces its own spontaneous aesthetic is the moral this book tries to draw. The polemics should not be dismissed as pale dilettantism because, in the final. analysis, aesthetics and economics are inalienably linked; beauty of form is a symbol of life-enhancement and therefore of survival.

What now are we to make of the so-called functional architecture of the international Modern Movement? Can this be regarded as life-enhancing?

Nor does it include such unfunctional delights as the decoration of ships, like the gilded baroque exuberance on the stern of the "Sovereign of the Seas" (detail from a painting by Lely), or the puffing putto on the rudder post of a botter seen on the Thames, or those surging pop-art spirits of the old wooden sailing ships – the figureheads.

10

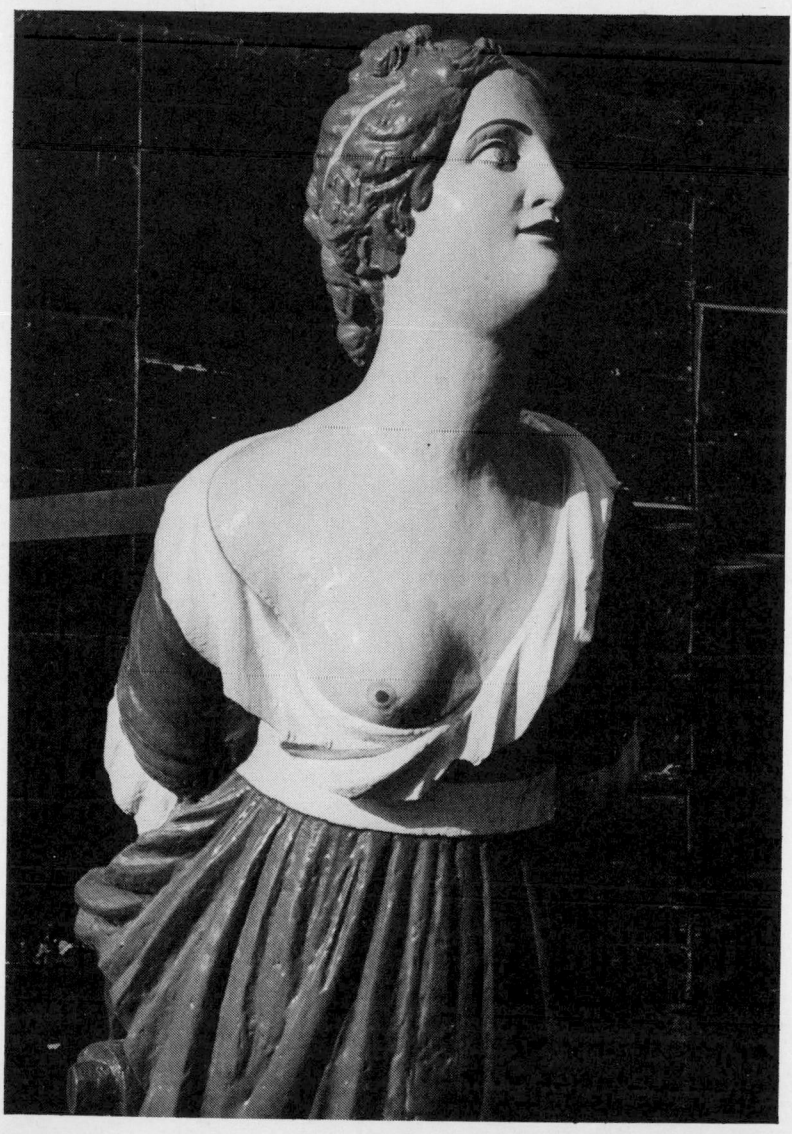

With its graceless brutality, its faceless, joyless inhumanity, its boring mechanical repetitions, and its monotonous machine-made surfaces (often hideously streaked because not even weathered), most modern architecture has become thoroughly discredited. The general view prevails, with good reason, that any proposed new building is certain to be worse than what it will replace.

In an article in the *Times Literary Supplement* for 23 February 1973, Mark Girouard wrote wisely: "In looking at professedly 'functional' buildings one has to distinguish between buildings that actually are functional and buildings that look functional . . . A whole language of symbolism has been worked out. Good lighting has been symbolised by abundance of glass, good heating by exposing the hot water pipes, good structure by exposing the concrete frame, good planning by expressing the internal arrangements in the external façades, and good economy by doing without ornament. This symbolic language can exist in a building that is subject to glare, expensive to heat, inefficiently constructed, inconveniently planned and expensive both to build and maintain. But the majority of critics have been prepared to accept the symbols for the reality, especially if they are used in a visually coherent way.*"

The UNESCO building in Paris is a blatant example. Over the past half-century the architectural laurels must not go to any architects but to a handful of masterly structural engineers.

Arrogant as architects tend to be in their vain efforts to become *divas,* and lacking as they do any common language with which to debate their activities with a bored and bemused public, they are perhaps less to blame for their many failures than either the laity or even they themselves believe. Willy-nilly they must do what their clients (mostly half-educated) pay them to do. Like everyone else, architects are the victims of a social-economic and therefore cultural situation for which everyone is finally responsible. Indeed, the solution to the whole environmental problem is obviously not in the end of a directly architectural nature; it is far wider and deeper. A culture acquires the environment it deserves, and in our own present state of technological barbarism we could do with more functional honesty in our economics (and thus in our philosophy) as well as in the plans and buildings they express.

Yet attempts must be made within the discontents to clarify architectural and planning principles because the environment itself conditions our lives: "We make our buildings and our buildings make us." One firm principle that must be revived, in opposition to mere formalism, is that of the genuine functionalism so strongly exemplified in the Nautical Style.

We also need to grow more aware of that life-denying element of puritanism that lies at the foundation of modern civilisation. This was certainly a force, if an unconscious one, behind the form-follows-function, machine-aesthetic revolt of the 'thirties. But, clearly, self-immolating austerity is not essential to the design of structures that work. These need not even exclude luxury; they certainly need not exclude joy, nor the pride of craftsmanship.

Anyway, it's nice to be beside the seaside. So let us return to our unadulterated muttons: the Nautical Style. Here we can view function free from modern perversions and inadequacies in an international style that has been disciplined by natural forces and by the limitations and possibilities implicit in materials, yet one which possesses, nevertheless, considerable freedom within these disciplines. The style can affect a whole neighbourhood with its character, as we can see in a number of old English

Nor naval uniforms, as revealed, for example, in this Staffordshire figure of a rating at the time of the Crimean War.

Nor functional bridges such as this delightful swinging example of timber on the Gloucester and Berkeley Canal.

12

Nor the gay curleycues on Victorian piers above deck, like this one at Brighton.

seaside towns. Lyme Regis in Dorset, with its monumental Cobb, is an outstanding case. And it can penetrate deep inland along canals and river navigations, as on the upper Thames of the Conservancy with its delightful, unique yet utterly functional and shipshape House Style which never becomes stereotyped: the great, solid timbers of its lock gates and

mooring posts, the delicate iron filligree of its weirs that so firmly control the water flow, its simple white fencing, its sculptural bollards and its elegant little timber footbridges across the weir streams, all painted pale grey and black and so contrasting brilliantly with the surrounding green of the verdure. Here along the Stream of Pleasure everything exists for a purpose and is in the right place to accomplish that purpose – a factor that adds to the soothing enjoyment of a river journey. Here too the surrounding ambience of the old riverside towns and villages as at Bray, Marlow and Henley is affected by this river style – an ambience that is both orderly and gay.

This term Nautical Style first appeared in a charming article by the painter, John Piper, printed in the *Architectural Review* as far back as January 1938. Since then a number of comments on the style has been proffered from time to time by the Architectural Press, this book being the latest – and probably the last. John Piper wrote as a visual artist who is intensely aware of the joyfulness inherent not only in good form *per se* but also in its textures, colours and tonal contrasts.

"There is a clear tradition of sea-coast building – particularly in England with its intense maritime pride and efficiency", he wrote in his article. "The tradition has a strong functional basis, and a vital one . . . Sailor's taste has always played its part in coast building: the lighthouse is an obvious example

Nor gleaming Georgian terrace houses by the sea such as these in Brunswick Square, Hove.

. . . Even lighthouse builders have never banished taste altogether from their buildings. This taste is quite indefinable, but it has qualities that can be named. The first is gaiety. In colour, for instance: stripes, spots, and a whole simple colour-symbolism belong to it – the gaiety that is reflected in sea shanties and in early naval prints (and in 'Sailors don't care'). The second quality is strength. Since a sailor has to depend on his boat for his life he never forgets, and sometimes exaggerates, the force of the wicked elements when he is building anything at all. The third quality is that of strong contrasts, more than half functional but partly tasteful . . . Above all these qualities there is a straightforwardness, an absence of *nuance;* but never an absence of romance . . .

"In general, two principles seem to have guided the nautical architect or engineer in considering his forms. First, the resistance of wind and water by turning them back or aside, and forming some kind of buttress against them. And secondly, the making of an open-work construction through which wind and water can whistle and blow and break without being offered too much resistance . . . Piers straddle the worst seas successfully with multiple spindle legs . . . Black, white and red are the colours that show up best on the sea, or from the sea: separately or combined. Fishermen tar their beach huts, where they keep their gear; partly from convenience because tar is handy, and partly so that

16

Nor Georgian custom houses, like the one at Poole.

Nor instruments for navigation, such as the binnacle of Brunel's "Great Eastern" steam ship as above. The examples of the Nautical Style that follow are restricted to purely functional structure.

they can see them on a bleached littoral when they come in from the sea in their boats. Trinity House often stripes its lighthouses in black and white or red and white. Low lights, harbour lights, groynes and jetties are kept a dazzling white or are thickly tarred, or have a wide red stripe on a shining white flank . . . Then there are those curious structures consisting of balls, and cones and cylinders hoisted on poles, that are used to warn shipping in a narrow harbour entrance that the channel is impassable; or to signal approaching storms . . .

"It would be far better to allow coastal gaiety to infect the whole country than let it be squeezed out by the inland habit. What there is of English seaside tradition should be preserved, and everyone responsible for developments to come should keep an eye on it . . . Strength, gaiety, geometry."

John Piper includes within his terms of reference not only Georgian custom houses with their classic porches and emblazoned coats of arms, but also the gleaming seaside terrace houses of Regency times with their pleasant bay windows and verandahs from which to observe ships passing or the changing moods of the sea. Of course these are part of the seaside *Stimmung* (English, strangely enough, lacks the right word), but here my own terms of reference exclude such buildings, just as they exclude waterway bridges, the curly decorations of Victorian piers above deck, navigational instruments, naval uniforms, and the design and loving decoration of

17

A collage of Newhaven by John Piper.

ships themselves – all of which could conceivably be included within the widest meaning of the term Nautical Style. In spite of the seductive delights of all maritime objects I have here stuck to my purely functional last in order the more firmly to articulate the argument. The last section, however, takes us to the borderline between land and water-borne structure. After that we shall be all aboard in the fascinating realm of ship-building – and that is another story.

Let the editorial comments of the *Architectural Review* for January 1950 summarise the matter: "Though examples of the Functional Tradition are to be found at every town throughout the countryside, it is at the seaboard that these are particularly strong. The forms peculiar to the maritime way of life, the jetties, piers, lighthouses, bollards, buoys, and a hundred other details demonstrate to a remarkable degree, not only the compelling requirements of this functional element, but also the freedom of form that is possible within the confines of this disciplinary code – the strict subservience to fundamentals which modern society in its complexity has to a large extent lost . . . The burden of technical awareness hangs heavily on the student and practising architect alike, and the sense of social responsibility often assumes the proportions and character of an incubus as well as a stimulant. A wholly satisfying, virile architecture cannot flourish unless in its practice social justification is lavishly compounded with personal pleasure . . . There is no need to regard such naïve delight as almost sinful or morally irresponsible, since without the ingredient of sensuous enjoyment the practice of architecture must inevitably degenerate into little more than a sordid routine, or at the most the exercise of mere intellectual cleverness . . . The pungent vitality and vernacular richness of the examples illustrated constitute a challenge to the architect . . . It is not a question of abandoning the machine but of mastering it before its drug-like influence has drained the vitality from the ordinary simple things that can mean so much."

In the spirit of the Nautical Style we can begin to see what the application of the genuine functional tradition, expressed in an honest, unaffected modern idiom, could contribute not only to individual buildings but to the total, detailed townscape of today. In the end we all love to ornament what we make, but first we must produce something worth ornamenting – something that works as beautifully, and looks as basically beautiful in form as a sea-wall, a pound lock, a lighthouse or a bollard.

High Water

High Water

Low Water

Low Water

20

2 SEA-WALLS, PIERS & HARBOURS

Sea-walls to keep the seas at bay, either to protect a sea front or to enclose a haven, must be as solid as rock. Sometimes, as on the jetty at Brighton shown here, the walls have projecting stones to break the force of the waves that beat against them – a lesson learned from nature.

Many sea-walls and harbours are of ancient origin and no one knows who built them or when they were built. The magnificent Cobb at Lyme Regis on the Dorset coast, which forms an artificial harbour on an exposed stretch of coast, is an example. Defoe mentions it as "a massy pile of building." It is a great work of stone, of a noble monumentality yet entirely functional with its free forms and virile sweeps and curves dictated by the position of the reef on which it is founded and by the need of a seaward face that carries the force of the waves away from the entrance. Its mile length shows a remarkable variety of surface tones, forms and textures. In comparison with the average marine parade with its dreary monotony, the Cobb has a salutary lesson to teach. Deservedly, it has been given the accolade as the Parthenon of the Functional Tradition.

Many harbours of more recent times have been engineered by men who are known and honoured. Thomas Telford, who devoted his life to improving communications for the ever-expanding economy of the Industrial Revolution, designed and built some two dozen harbours in Scotland, notably at Aberdeen and Dundee. These are solid works designed with care and precision to accomplish arduous jobs of protection.

The sturdy granite sea-wall of Aberdeen Harbour under construction, an engraving from Atlas to the Life of Thomas Telford *(1838).*

Timber. Left, the breakwater at Holyhead on the occasion of a visit by Brunel's fabulous "Great Eastern" (Illustrated London News, 1859). Below, the wall of stone and timber at Esbjerg, Denmark.

Iron and stone. Left, the forest of
ironwork supporting Blackpool Pier.
Strength is gained by a kind of
structural judo whereby the force of wind
and waves is allowed to by-pass through
the skeleton. Time adds its decorative
touches in adhering molluscs and
seaweed. Right, a solid jetty at Brighton
where a man-made construction borrows
an idea from nature: projecting stones
help to break the force of the waves like
the preservative flints embedded in a
chalk cliff.

Left, St. Ives Harbour at low tide with its tapered rock-like walls of stone sculptured with steps and decorated with small lighthouses. Below, a sloping sea-wall somewhere in England with delicate iron railings serving as a foil to the heavy stonework. Right, the sea-wall at Sandgate protects the front, wavering in its lines like a sea serpent but indomitably indestructible.

On this and facing page, aspects of the Cobb, Lyme Regis. Of unknown age, its plan is free in form but utterly functional; full of interesting sweeps and curves and rich in its variety and vitality of surfaces, tones and textural patterns – like those of natural objects. Here the functional tradition is on a splendid scale. Right, an approach to the Cobb, with a slim and useful railing, a simple minimal affair of tubing that follows the irregular contours of the sea-wall, giving first a visual and then a tactile warning.

3 WAREHOUSES, DOCKS & SPECIAL STRUCTURES

As well as protected harbours, the nineteenth century produced a great number of enclosed, lock-controlled docks surrounded by multi-storeyed warehouses "buylded after gorgious and gallante sort." Liverpool, for example, has its Albert Dock of red brick, granite and iron; designed by Jesse Hartley, it was opened in 1845 as the finest dock group in the country – an immensely impressive work.

During the nineteenth century too, London acquired a number of new enclosed docks along the river banks below the Tower. They were badly needed to overcome the congestion on the river as well as to protect cargoes from the weather, from pilfering and from smuggling; they also allowed ships to float on even keels in deep water beside the quays whatever the state of the tide might be on the river itself.

Some indication of the simple, dramatic and yet entirely functional quality of these commercial docks and warehouses can still be gained from what remains of them today with their towering, fortress-like outer walls so solid and strong that they possess that sense of indestructibility which is the essence of monumentality. Gustave Doré conveys their mysterious, fortress-like character in his famous engravings for *London: A Pilgrimage* published in 1872.

The naval dockyards also offer fine examples. At Sheerness stands a building of considerable historical importance (as Professor A. W. Skempton of the Imperial College pointed out after the author had discovered it on a roving commission in 1956). Completed in 1860 this is the first multi-storey iron-framed structure in existence – father of the steel-framed skyscrapers of New York and a prototype of modern frame-and-fill architecture. It is quite functional and surprisingly modern in appearance with its clearly expressed trabeation of H-sections. With new materials and methods, it follows the old tradition of the reasonable, unselfconscious style of the millwright and the shipwright.

Three modern examples of waterside structures for varied purposes which also maintain the tradition and are as crisp and rational as the Sheerness Boat Store close this chapter.

Left, detail from one of Gustave Doré's evocative engravings in London: A Pilgrimage *of dockland with its high cliffs of brick warehouses that surrounded the enclosed docks before steam had ousted sail.*

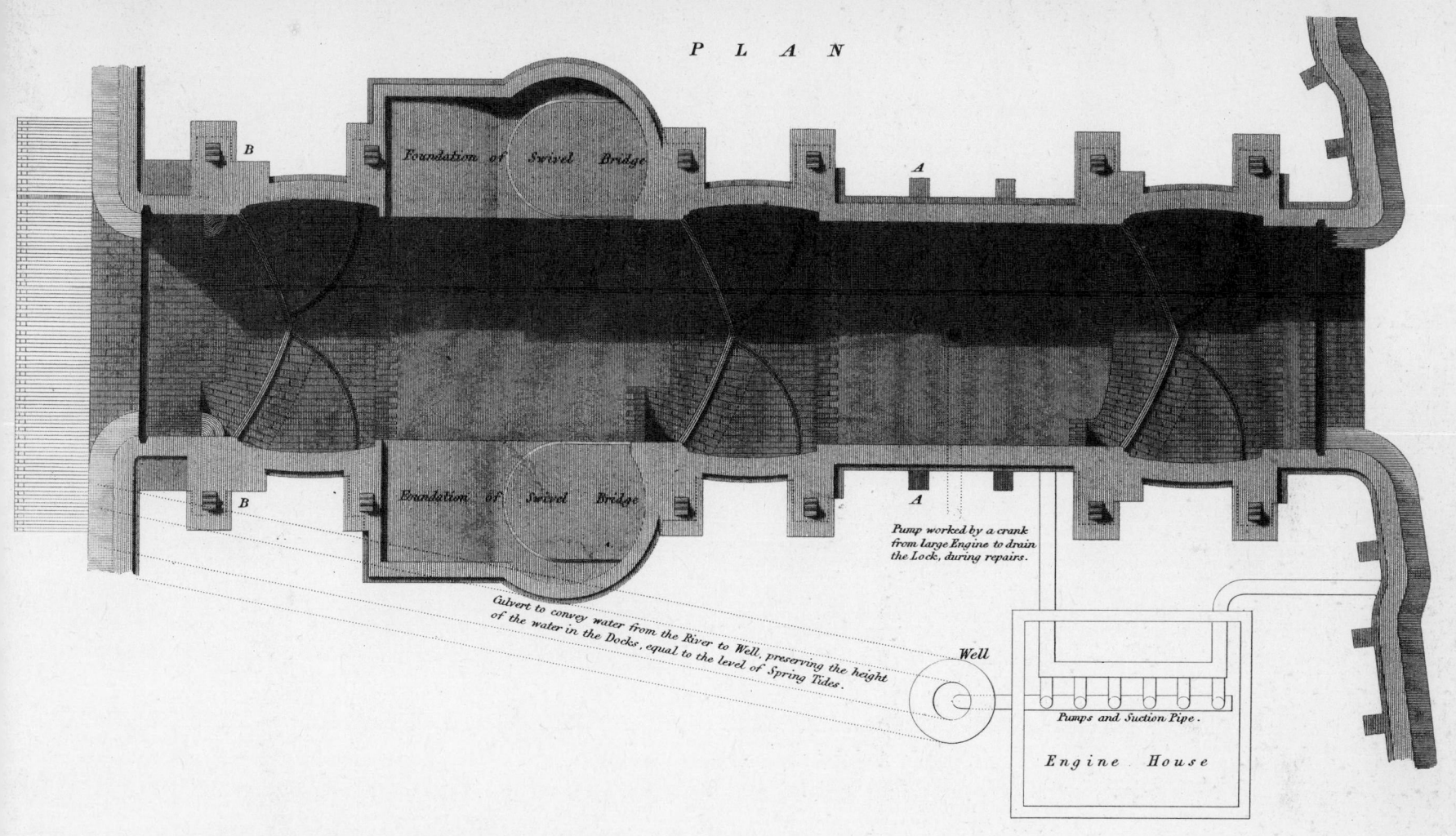

PLAN

B

Foundation of Swivel Bridge

A

B

Foundation of Swivel Bridge

A

Pump worked by a crank
from large Engine to drain
the Lock, during repairs.

Culvert to convey water from the River to Well, preserving the height
of the water in the Docks, equal to the level of Spring Tides.

Well

Pumps and Suction Pipe.

Engine House

Left, Doré's view of an interior of St. Katherine Dock showing
its functional fire-proof construction of brick floors and iron
columns. Above, an engraving from Telford's Atlas of the plan
of the entrance lock to St. Katherine Dock, with its visually
satisfying but essentially functional lines and forms.

33

Timber produces its own character in structure
by reason of its inherent limitations and
qualities, notably as wall coverings in the form
of boarding that makes a distinctive texture of
parallel lines. And it needs protection with
paint or tar. Left, old warehouses at Rye, all
tarred, with some lower walling of brickwork.
Above, ventilated stores at Chatham Naval
Dockyard. Right, grand wooden warehouses at
Trondheim, Norway, on stilts of logs with
walls painted in bright, variegated colours;
though the windows are mostly rhythmical,
some appear in seemingly arbitrary places
which must in fact be where they are most
needed.

Brick and stone produce their own vernacular. Left, the
Quadrangle, Sheerness Dockyard, with plain clock tower of
timber and great arched entrance surrounded by stone trim. In
the foreground are typical elements of the Nautical Style: stone
steps to the water articulated along their sides by white paint,
a black-and-white bollard, thin tubular railings and a simple
barrier of posts and chains. Above, two views of the majestic
Albert Dock, Liverpool, completed in 1845 in red brick,
granite trim, giant Doric columns made of iron, and fireproof
construction of iron frame and brick-vaulted floors. The
vocabulary includes rounded brick corners, granite for setts,
plinths and bollards, and a rhythm of great elliptical arches
every fourth bay.

Left, a red brick warehouse at Poole, well textured by weathering and use, the reveal of a door whitewashed for articulation and increase of light within. Right, a terrace of nineteenth-century warehouses at Liverpool, powerful in scale and, while showing some architectural pretensions, quite functional in fact.

The Boat Store, Sheerness (formerly a naval dockyard) is a remarkable structure of great importance in the history of building, for it is the earliest multi-storey iron-framed edifice in existence. Surprisingly its date of completion is as long ago as 1860, although it is quite modern in looks. Its designer was Colonel Godfrey T. Greene, Director of the Admiralty's Engineering and Architectural Works. Left, a general view, and, right, four of its iron details that reveal a very early use of the H-section. The junctions are carefully and elegantly conceived in a logical and precise manner.

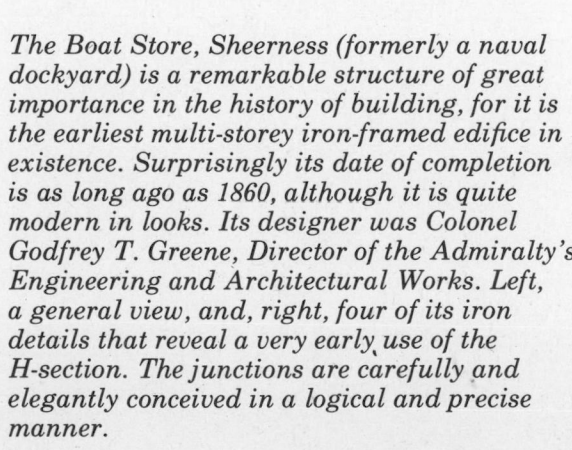

Three modern examples of the Nautical Style applied to waterside buildings. Left, a coastguard tower on Southampton Water, 100 feet high, built for the Department of the Environment in 1972. The tower, 6 feet in diameter, is topped by a control room and look-out with gallery access to a radar scanner. (Designer: E. Solley, Regional Civil Engineer, DoE). Below, a perky little starter's box for sailing races by the Thames, erected for the Hammersmith Borough Council. Designed by A. W. Rodmell, Borough Engineer and Surveyor, it won a Civic Trust award in 1964. Right, the Grafham Sailing Club, Diddington Reservoir, Hunts., is a cleanly functional design with a reinforced concrete frame. It provides among its amenities panoramic views both from within and from the commodious roof deck, as well as a starter's box like a glass-house on a pole. Gaiety is here with white-and-black, glittering glass and fluttering flags. The ground floor is set back to provide a protected area for summer parties. (Architects: Robert Matthew, Johnson-Marshall and Partners.)

4 LIGHTHOUSES

Lighthouses go back a long way – at least to 260 B.C. when Ptolemy II erected the Pharos, 400 feet high, at Alexandria, one of the Seven Wonders of the World. At its top a fire burned at night, and this form of lighting using wood or coal prevailed right up to the last century, by which time candles, oil, acetylene gas and finally electricity were generally being used, the light being directed by reflectors and glass lenses.

Great skill and care has, of necessity, been lavished on the construction of lighthouses, for they have to defy not only the assaults of high winds but often of waves that can in storms exert a pressure of more than 4,000 lbs. per square foot. Thus they tend to display a massive simplicity that produces, without intent, a monumental type of architecture. (The ancient lighthouses of Libya were indeed treated as temples as well as utilities.)

The archetype, and perhaps the most famous lighthouse in the world, is Smeaton's Eddystone. It stood fourteen miles south-west of Plymouth Harbour until re-erected at Plymouth Hoe as a monument to its designer when a new and similar structure (designed by Sir James Douglass) took over in 1884. Smeaton's fine design, the third on this dangerous sloping rock, was begun in 1756 and lasted for well over a century, thanks to the solid dovetailed, toggled, plugged and cemented stonework, hyperbolic form and broad base. In the end it was not Smeaton's cohesive monolith that gave way but the rock beneath it. Its building, in which blocks of stone weighing up to three tons had to be manipulated in the dangerous waters, took just over three years to accomplish, although only sixteen weeks' work on the rock itself had been possible during that time.

Besides the Eddystone, a number of other well-known lighthouses are illustrated here, as well as some small ones that are little known. Whether famous or obscure, all lighthouses are the purest exemplars of the functional Nautical Style.

Left, John Smeaton's Edystone Lighthouse in a storm, the dramatic title-page engraving to his great folio of 1813: A Narrative of the Building and a Description of the Construction of the Edystone Lighthouse with Stone. *Smeaton describes the scene thus: "At intervals of a minute, and sometimes two or three; I suppose when a combination happens to produce one overgrown wave, it would strike the rock and the building conjointly, and fly up in a white column, enwrapping it like a sheet, rising at least to double the height of the house, and totally intercepting it from sight." The house stood for over 120 years, before the rock itself gave way, so firm and functional was its design.*

45

Three early lighthouses: left, Harwich, built in 1801, is somewhat "architectural" in its details but has a basic, simple, geometrical form; it might, indeed, be dubbed a functional folly or eye-catcher that enlivens a townscape. Below, St. Agnes on the Scilly Isles built in 1690 to burn coal as a light. Right, the chantry lighthouse erected in 1323 by Walter de Godyton on St. Catherine's Down on the Isle of Wight, the earliest surviving lighthouse in the British Isles, a simple, indestructible, functional affair of stone.

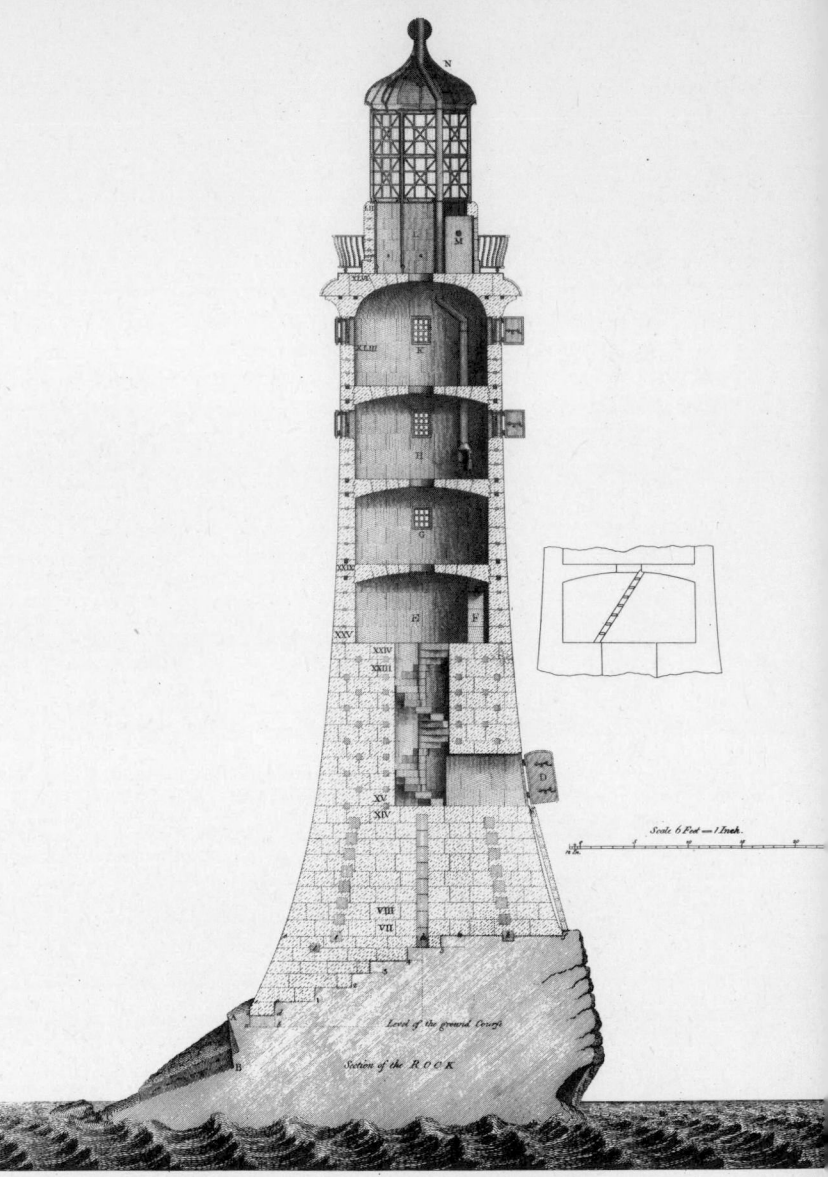

South ELEVATION *of the* STONE LIGHTHOUSE *completed upon the* EDYSTONE *in 1759.*

Shewing the Prospect of the nearest Land, as it appears from the Rocks in a clear calm Day.

Engraved in the Year 1763, by Mr. Edw.d Rooker. The figures by Mr. Sam.l Wale.

SECTION *of the* EDYSTONE LIGHTHOUSE *upon the* E *&* W *Line, as relative to N.º 8.*

on Supposition of its being LOW WATER *of a* SPRING TIDE.

Engraved in the Year 1763, by Mr. Edw.d R.

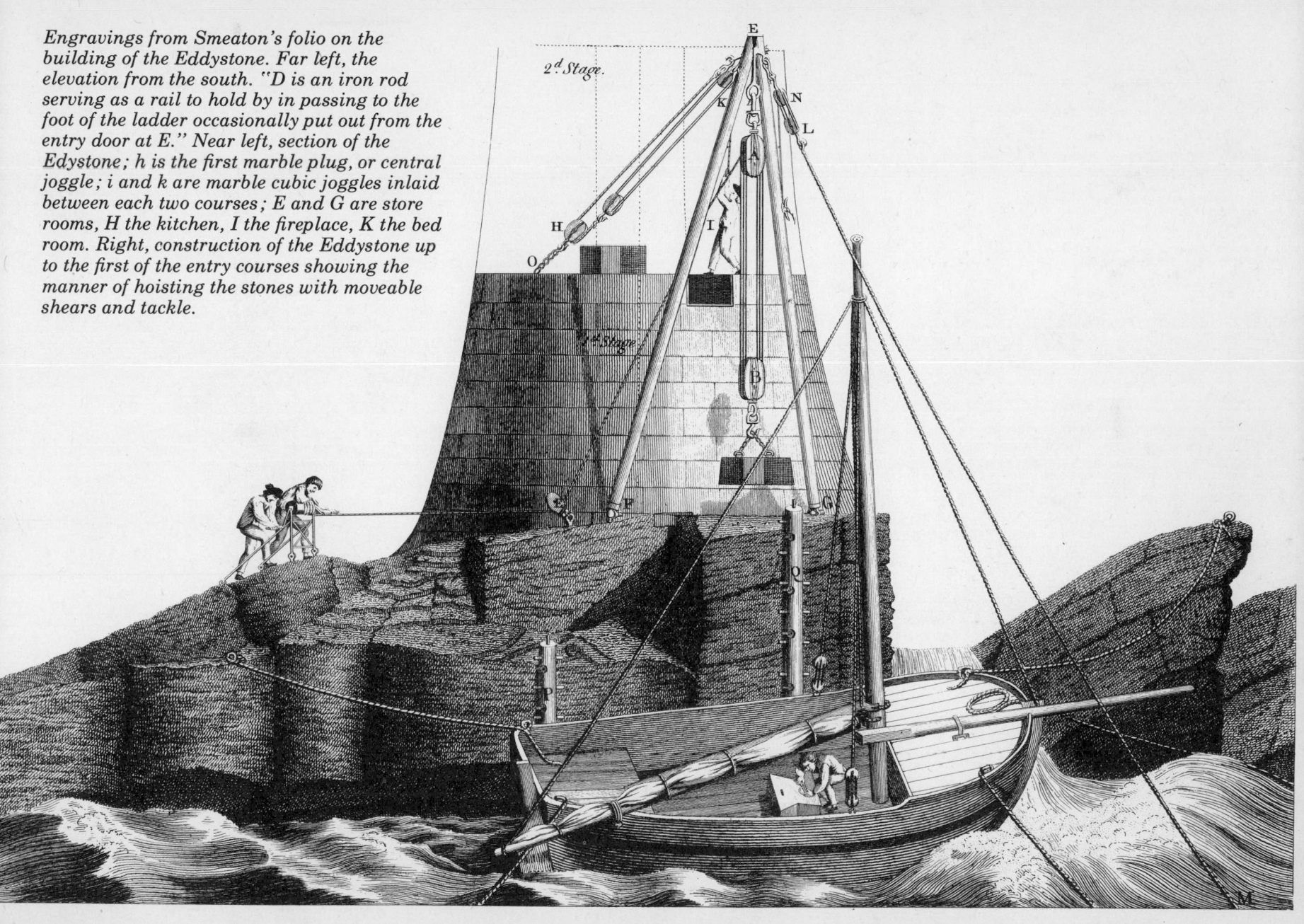

Engravings from Smeaton's folio on the building of the Eddystone. Far left, the elevation from the south. "D is an iron rod serving as a rail to hold by in passing to the foot of the ladder occasionally put out from the entry door at E." Near left, section of the Edystone; h is the first marble plug, or central joggle; i and k are marble cubic joggles inlaid between each two courses; E and G are store rooms, H the kitchen, I the fireplace, K the bed room. Right, construction of the Eddystone up to the first of the entry courses showing the manner of hoisting the stones with moveable shears and tackle.

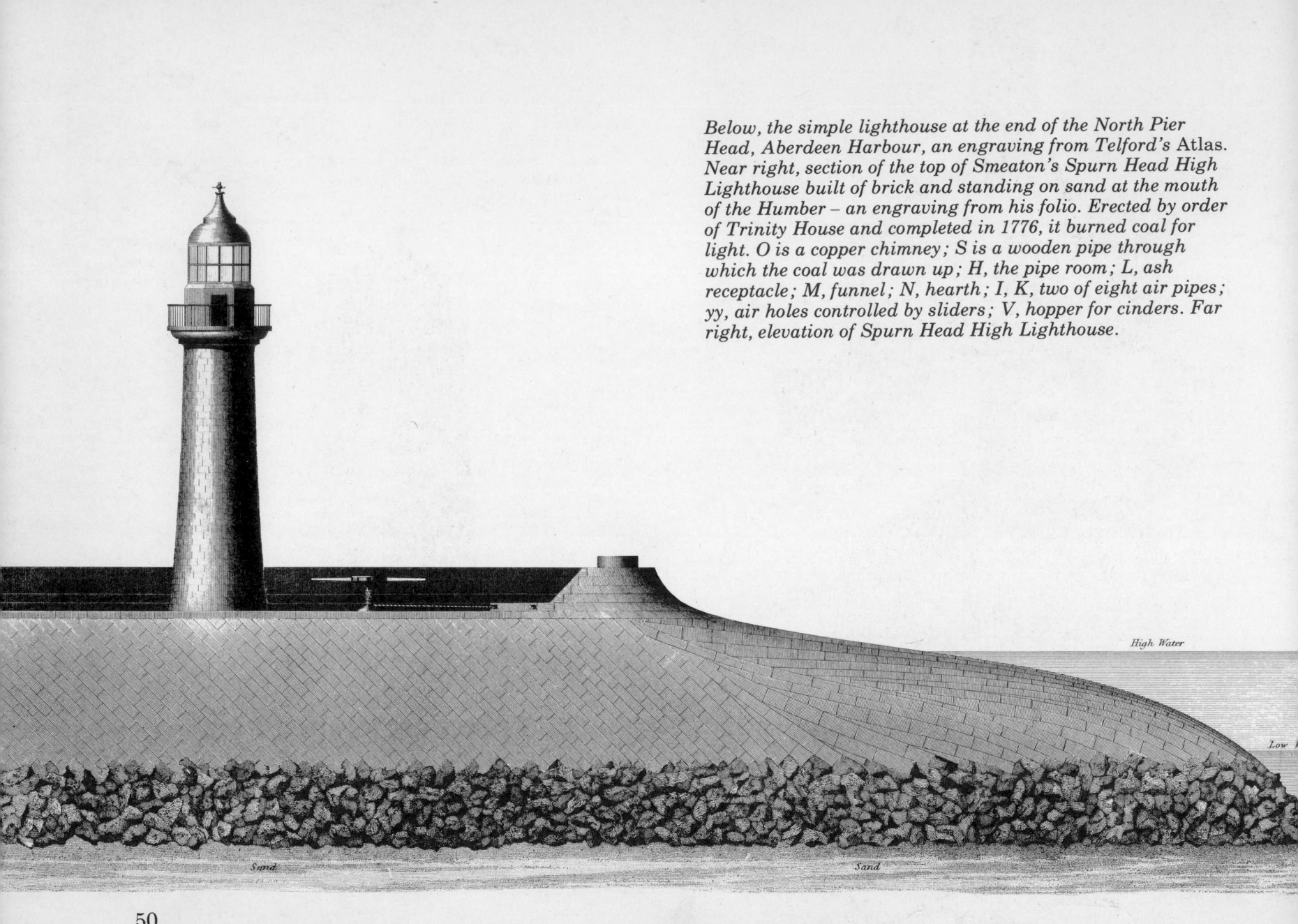

Below, the simple lighthouse at the end of the North Pier Head, Aberdeen Harbour, an engraving from Telford's Atlas. Near right, section of the top of Smeaton's Spurn Head High Lighthouse built of brick and standing on sand at the mouth of the Humber – an engraving from his folio. Erected by order of Trinity House and completed in 1776, it burned coal for light. O is a copper chimney; S is a wooden pipe through which the coal was drawn up; H, the pipe room; L, ash receptacle; M, funnel; N, hearth; I, K, two of eight air pipes; yy, air holes controlled by sliders; V, hopper for cinders. Far right, elevation of Spurn Head High Lighthouse.

High Water

Low W

Sand

Sand

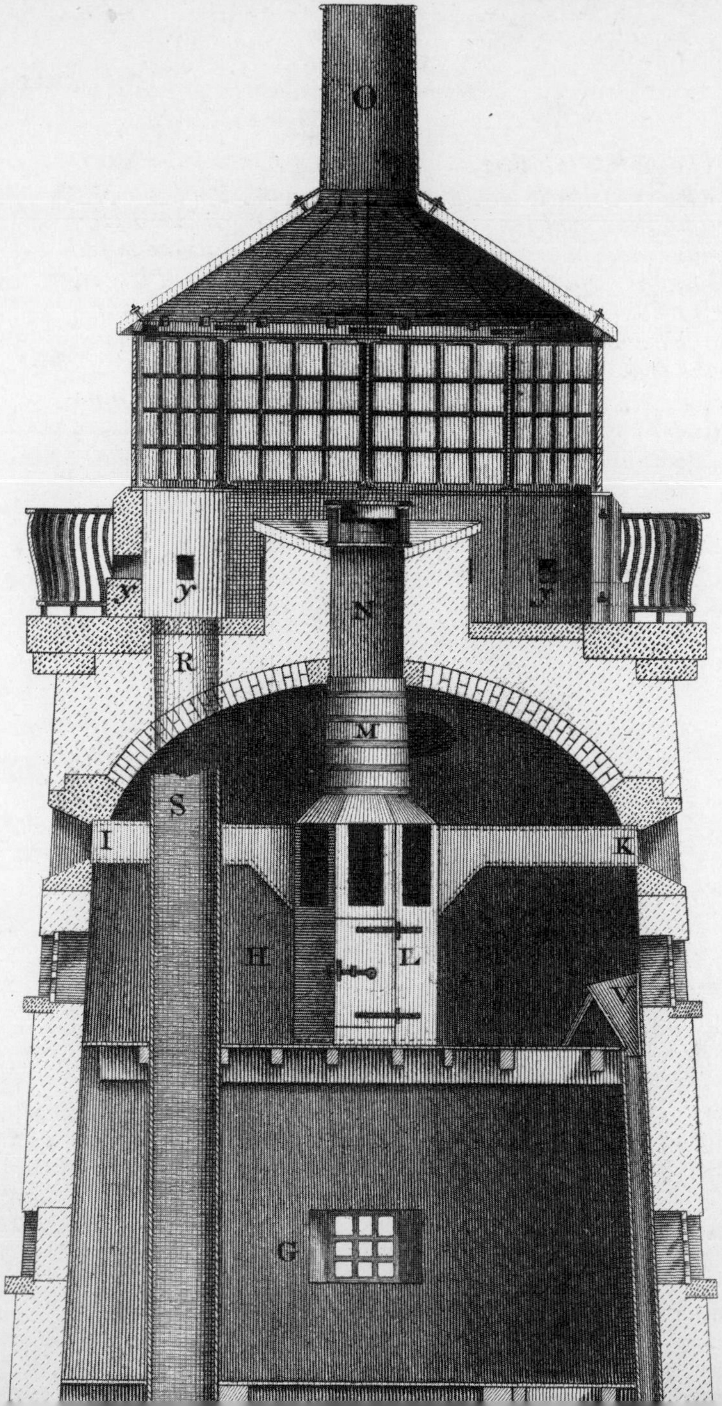

51

Left, this little timber lighthouse on the shore of Lake Vänern in central Sweden is painted white as a marker against the dark pinewood by day; it reveals the Nautical Style in its most exquisite and unselfconscious simplicity. In the next few pages a litter of lighthouses, all British. Right: Start Point, Devon.

Southwold, Suffolk.

Flamborough, Yorkshire.

St. Anne's, Pembrokeshire.

Needles, Isle of Wight.

Burnham, Somerset.

Left, St. Catherine's on the southern tip of the Isle of Wight, has a mildly stylistic flavour with its castellations and corbel dentils, but essentially it is an adapted and functional complex of character. The main tower was built in 1838 of ashlar stone as a high three-tier octagon but in 1875 this was reduced in height to avoid the mist caps; a fog signal was mounted in an attached tower in 1932, so giving rise to the local title, the Cow and the Calf. Right, the new automatic Dungeness Lighthouse built for Trinity House and completed in 1960 to the design of Ronald Ward and Partners. Some sort of light has existed here at least since 1600 and in the distance the earlier house of 1904 can be seen. The tower of the new house is unusual in having no taper, for it is built of pre-cast, pre-stressed concrete rings with additional reinforcement towards the base. It contains the most up-to-date electronic equipment, a radio beacon and a fog horn audible six miles out at sea. The spiral ramp contains the equipment but, in a functional lapse, it does not lead to the entrance but is merely a promenade. Below, a view from the tower.

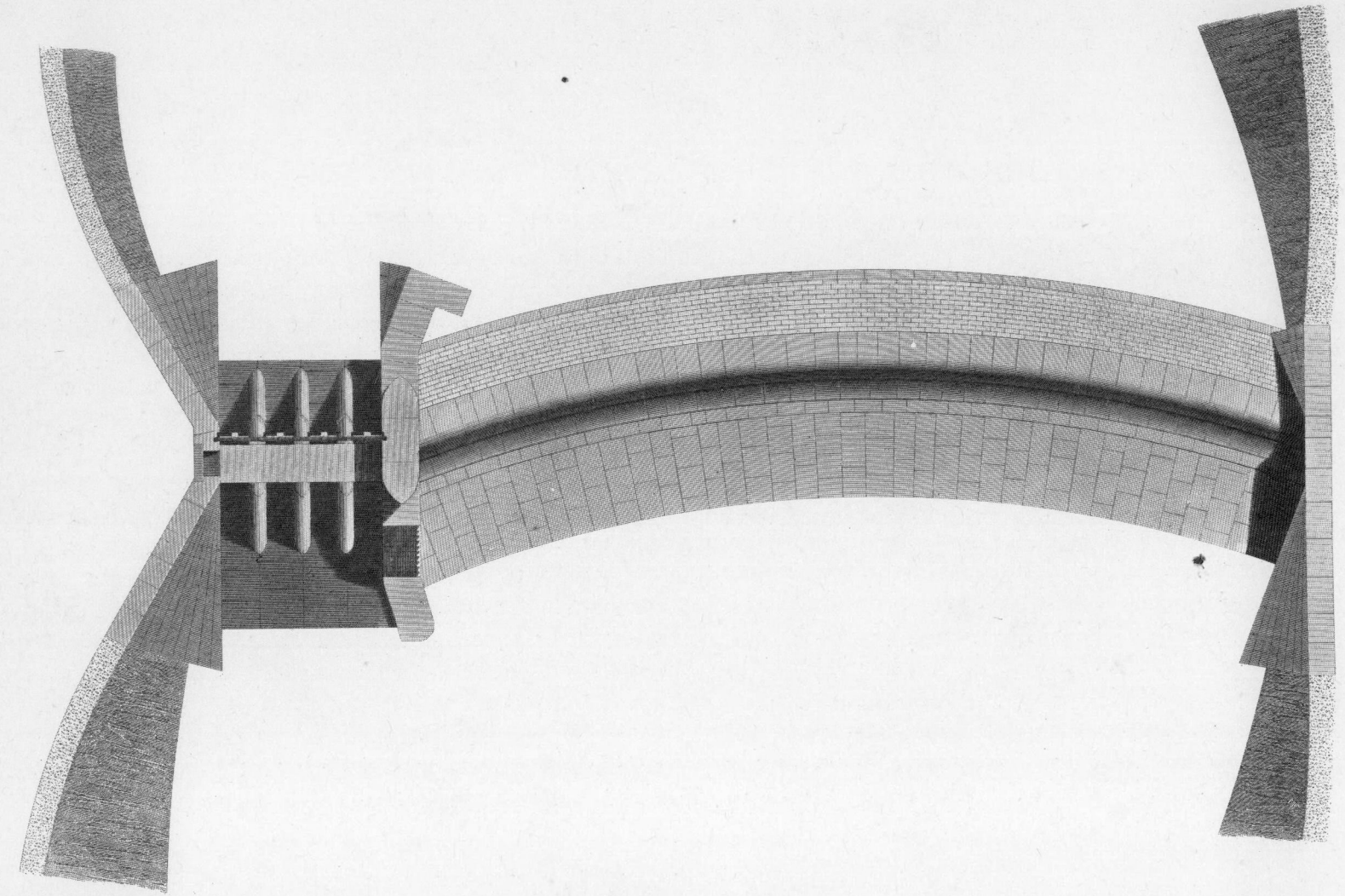

60

5 ON INLAND WATERS

The idiom of the seaboard appears in modified forms in the more protected waters of rivers and canals – in the solid brick warehouse, in the shipyard and slipway, in waterside furniture such as the mooring ring, the row of bollards, the weir machinery, and, most notably, in the retaining sides of the pound lock that recall the solid barriers of sea-walls. The orderliness of Sailor's Taste is here too, as well as the clarity and strength of functional design in general.

The two most important elements of any navigation, whether an artificial cut or a canalised river, are the weirs and the locks which control the descending flow of water. The primitive flash lock was merely a dam in which a gate for the passage of water or a boat was fixed. This could cause serious loss of precious water in dry seasons, besides being hazardous for navigation. The pound lock solved the problem by restricting a reach of water or pound to a short length that could just accommodate the largest craft likely to use the navigation; in the pound boats could be raised or lowered in a small volume of water by opening or closing sluices fixed in the gates, or at their sides, at either end of the lock.

The invention of the pound lock has often been attributed to Leonardo da Vinci; in fact it was first used in China nearly a millenium ago. With its solid retaining walls and sturdy gates (with great cantilevered beams when manually worked), with its steps and changes of level, together with the weir like a man-made waterfall, spidery cat walk and beautiful sluice machinery – the lock among the most visually satisfying objects in the Nautical Style.

Their character percolates into waterside towns and villages, and this could be deliberately applied today in new waterside developments – as Gordon Cullen has shown in his brilliant drawings, three of which appear in the following pages.

Plan of Saltersford Weir on the Weaver Navigation, one of the fine engravings in Telford's Atlas.

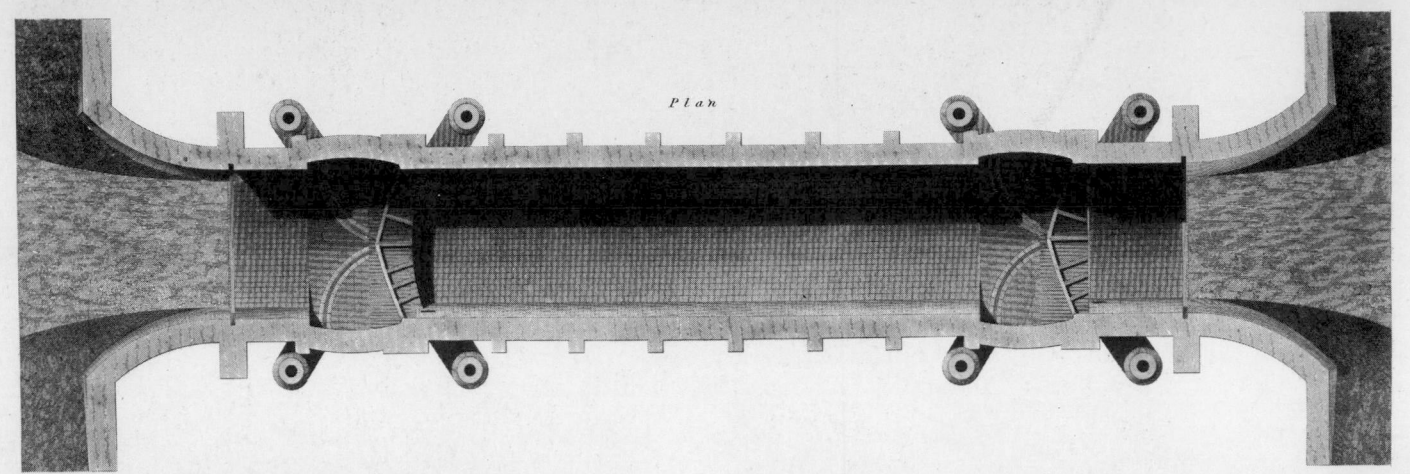

Plan

Canal locks. Top left, a plan for a lock on the Caledonian Canal (from Telford's Atlas). Bottom far left, a lock on the Staffordshire and Worcestershire Canal showing how the Narrow Boat just fits so that no precious water is wasted. Bottom near left, a staircase of locks on the Welsh section of the Shropshire Union Canal. Above, capstan machinery for opening and shutting lock gates (Telford's Atlas). Right, a ship lock on the Göta Canal, Sweden, with great steel gates worked by electric power.

Thames locks. Left, a Victorian engraving of a flash lock on the upper river. Below, two modern pound locks. Right, a lock gate whose massive timbers form an intricate pattern of light and shade.

Thames weirs. Left, an iron weir, a complex of essential parts which, by chance, produce ornamental effects. Below left, a weir of wood. Below right, a weir of wood and steel.

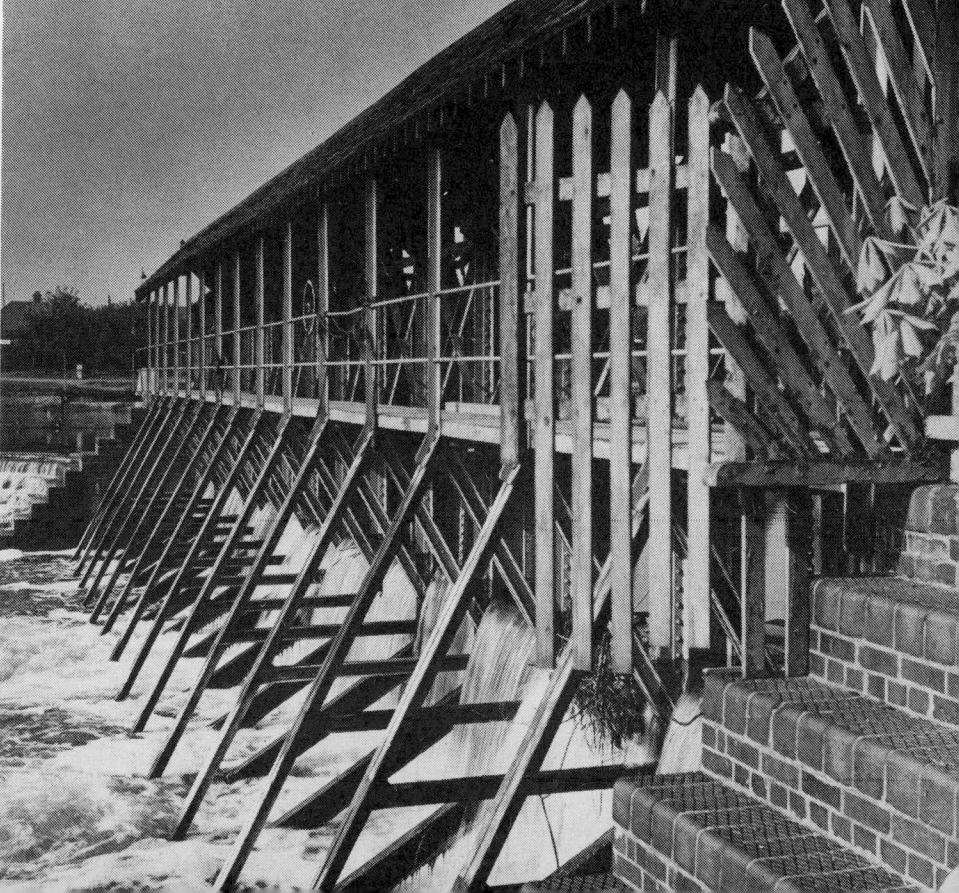

The Nautical Style applied to townscape in the
imagination of Gordon Cullen. Left, The South Bank
between Blackfriars and London Bridge.
Centre, A riverside walk along the river front below
Upper Thames Street, showing how a maritime
atmosphere might be introduced. Right, A water
street in the project for the Town of New Marlow on
the Thames with a gay holiday air, picturesque
complexity, variety of levels, glittering reflections
and general bustle.

68

6 SCULPTURE BY ACCIDENT

The smaller artifacts required by water transport display the same strength and firmness of form as the larger structures. The eyes can enjoy them for their own formal sake as unintended pieces of sculpture that create focal points of interest to decorate the maritime scene: derricks, cranes, hoists, buoys, signals, sluice and lock machinery and, above all, bollards with their infinite variety of shapes in wood, stone or iron made simply to rope a craft firmly to its quayside mooring.

This is Poor Man's Sculpture, or Sculpture by Accident, which could – indeed perhaps already has – provided inspiration for some sophisticated modern sculptors in search of significant form. It is part of the decor of the Nautical Style. It is also, in one sense, architecture, in that architecture has three visual meanings: the two-dimensional meaning of the façade and the wall, the three-dimensional meaning when a structure is seen externally and can be circumambulated like a piece of sculpture, and the four-dimensional meaning of internal spatial control where time is involved because it can only be appreciated by the wandering body. (This last aspect of architecture, although "internal", can be appreciated in a town as well as in a single building, in that one wanders along through streets which are corridors, and emerges into open places which are rooms, the sky serving as ceiling.)

This latter four-dimensional aspect of architecture can hardly be conveyed on a two-dimensional surface, and the pictures in this book must inevitably be restricted to the first and second categories: façade and three-dimensional form, or sculpture – whether in a whole structure or in a small detail like a buoy or a bollard. The whole Nautical Style, in fact, tends to limit itself to the three-dimensional, external, sculptural aspect of architecture – not least in small objects of an obviously sculptural quality that contribute much to the whole nautical scene.

This floating derrick of iron for lifting wrecks had a purely functional purpose; yet it forms a grand piece of abstract sculpture that might not seem out of place today on the roof of the Hayward Gallery in London (Illustrated London News, 1859).

Buoys, those useful but beautiful objects with their bright colours and distinctive forms painted with rings, chequers and stripes, have been in use since the eleventh century. The big breakthrough did not come, however, until the middle of the last century with the addition of warning lights and sound signals such as bells. Far left, the interior of the Buoy Store, Trinity Wharf, Blackwall, and, above, the exterior of the store where two light vessels can be seen in the background (Illustrated London News, 1868). The Wharf was the main depot of the ancient Corporation of Trinity House that controls the lights and buoys of our coasts.

73

More sculptural objects made for the sake of safety. Left, geometry at the Harbour Master's stores, Cowes. Below, a life buoy on the Thames. Right, a pattern of signals at Esbjerg Harbour, Denmark.

This bloom of bollards indicate the immense richness in shapes and textures – whether in wood, stone or iron – these objects of utility reveal. Each one is a personage.

*Old iron for nautical use. Left, a
mooring ring. Right, an anchor chain.*

DUNDEE GRAVING DOCK.

Transverse Section.

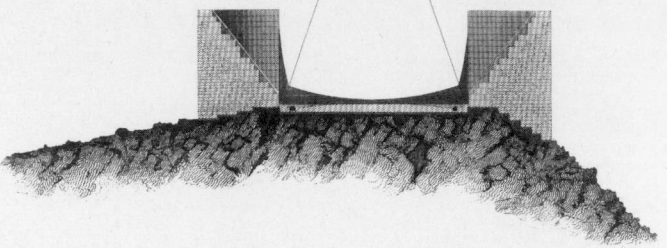

Longitudinal Section.

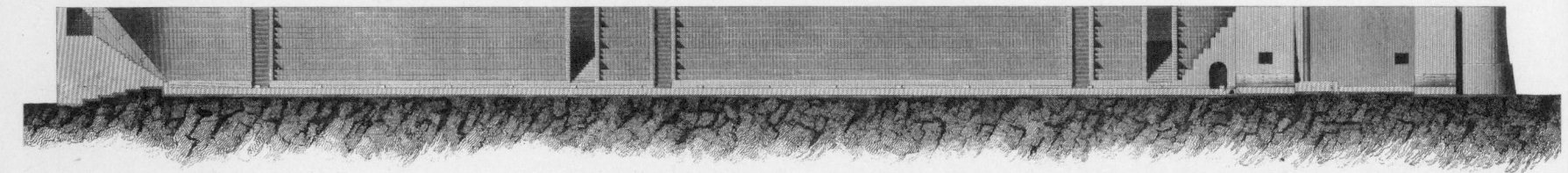

P L A N

Scale of Feet

10 5 0   10   20   30   40   50   60   70   80   90   100

7 WHERE BOATS & BUILDINGS MEET

In spite of its seductiveness, ship design has been avoided in this book. Yet an area exists where maritime structures and ships embrace – where the architecture of land and of water overlap or conjoin, where builder and shipwright either co-operate or borrow ideas – and even actual constructions – from each other, and where the works of both remain, nevertheless, within the Nautical Style.

Here, finally, are illustrated a few bold examples: a graving dock wherein a ship can be washed and brushed up – shipyard towers of skeletal steelwork – a monumental launching cradle – old Peggotty-type boats turned upside down to keep out the rain from above instead of the sea from below – a drawing room afloat that bravely tries to retain the stability of land – and that most functional and physiologically satisfying of vernacular units ever designed: the so-called Georgian sash window applied to the sterns of ships – a commodious summer house afloat on the river – a mediaeval land castle built for battles at sea – and a room in a modern Grand Babylon hotel designed for a ship that crosses the ocean.

And here, in conclusion, and for good measure, is a vivid picture in words, describing no luxury hotel but a primitive, functional but cosy aedicule, a one-room flat for a small commune that goes to sea. It can be found on the opening page of Pierre Loti's *Iceland Fisherman*:

"The den tapered towards one end, like the interior of a great hollow sea-gull ... Outside, no doubt, was the sea and the night, but there was little or no indication of this within: a single opening cut in the roof was closed by a wooden lid, and the light came from an old hanging lamp which swung slowly ... Their massive table occupied the whole of the room, conforming exactly to its shape, and there remained just room to get round in order to sit on the shallow lockers fixed to the oaken walls. Large beams passed above them, almost touching their heads; and behind their backs, sleeping berths, which seemed to have been hollowed out of the

Plan and sections of Dundee Graving Dock (Telford's Atlas).

thickness of the timber, opened like the niches of a vault for the dead. All the woodwork was massive and defaced, impregnated with dampness and sea salt; worn, polished by the rubbings of their hands . . . They had been drinking wine and cider out of their bowls, and the joy of physical well-being brightened their faces which were open and honest. Very close to one another, for want of space, they seemed to be enjoying a great sense of ease, talking thus in their little room. Outside, no doubt, was the sea and the night, the infinite desolation of dark and profound waters."

The upturned husks of Holy Island, off the Northumbrian coast, have retired to land after a life-time's service as colliers and bulk carriers to serve in old age as fishermen's sheds, attractive still in their weather-beaten dignity.

*Left, a launching cradle at Liverpool indicates the dramatic
architectural scale that maritime structures can produce.
Right, a shipyard on the Clyde with its complexity of towers,
cranes and other steel structures.*

Left, the drawing-room goes to sea: a device invented by Sir Henry Bessemer who suffered severely from sea-sickness. Its aim was to stabilise part of a passenger ship by pivoting the saloon on a central bearing and controlling it with an hydraulic levelling apparatus (Illustrated London News, 1875). The ship was built to speed between Dover and Calais in one hour. Though it was a brave effort to achieve a specific function, the saloon, which was very grand in its decorations, seems to have worked only with moderate success and no other example was built.

Above, the mediaeval castle goes to sea: a woodcut from De Re Militari by Robert Valturious (Verona, 1472, the first printed book with technical illustrations). The castles erected fore and aft were applied much earlier.

Right, the Georgian window, that most functional of building units, went to sea in ships like Nelson's "Victory".

*Above, the summer house takes to water: an engraving from
The Book of the Thames (c. 1860). Right, the modern luxury
hotel takes to the ocean: part of a suite in the "Queen
Elizabeth 2" designed by Buzas and Irvine. A rich but
functional interior where only the portholes indicate that this
is on board a liner.*